GW00713290

Leslie Kenton is an award-winning writer, novelist, teacher, social activist and bestselling author of more than thirty books. A well-known TV broadcaster and the daughter of jazz musician Stan Kenton, Leslie has spent more than twenty-five years working in the realms of health, philosophy and the exploration of consciousness. She first became famous for books such as *Raw Energy* and *Ageless Ageing*, which have been translated into many languages. For fourteen years she was an editor for *Harpers & Queen*.

Author's Note

The material in this book is intended for information purposes only. None of the suggestions or information is meant in any way to be prescriptive. Any attempt to treat a medical condition should always come under the directions of a competent medical practitioner – and neither the publisher nor I can accept responsibility for injuries or illness arising out of a failure by a reader to take medical advice. I am only a reporter. I also have a profound interest in helping myself and others to maximise our potential for positive health which includes being able to live at a high level of energy, intelligence and creativity. For all three are expressions of harmony within a living organic system.

Also by Leslie Kenton

THE JOY OF BEAUTY
ULTRAHEALTH
RAW ENERGY (with Susannah Kenton)
RAW ENERGY RECIPES (with Susannah Kenton)
AGELESS AGEING
THE BIOGENIC DIET
10 DAY CLEAN-UP PLAN
CELLULITE REVOLUTION
ENDLESS ENERGY (with Susannah Kenton)
NATURE'S CHILD
LEAN REVOLUTION
10 DAY DE-STRESS PLAN
THE NEW JOY OF BEAUTY
THE NEW ULTRAHEALTH
THE NEW AGELESS AGEING
THE NEW BIOGENIC DIET

THE NEW RAW ENERGY (with Susannah Kenton)
PASSAGE TO POWER
RAW ENERGY FOOD COMBINING DIET
JUICE HIGH (with Russell Cronin)
TEN STEPS TO ENERGY
TEN STEPS TO A YOUNGER YOU
THE RAW ENERGY BIBLE
TEN STEPS TO A NEW YOU

QUICK FIX SERIES
Chill Out
Kick Colds
Juice Blitz

Fiction
LUDWIG (a spiritual thriller)

Leslie Kenton
DETOX NOW

Vermilion · London

1 3 5 7 9 10 8 6 4 2

First published in the United Kingdom in 2000 by Vermilion, an imprint of Random House
20 Vauxhall Bridge Road · London SW1V 2SA

Random House Australia (Pty) Limited
20 Alfred Street · Milsons Point · Sydney · New South Wales 2061 · Australia

Random House New Zealand Limited
18 Poland Road · Glenfield · Auckland 10 · New Zealand

Random House South Africa (Pty) Limited
Endulini · 5a Jubilee Road · Parktown 2193 · South Africa

Random House Group Limited Reg. No. 954009

A CIP catalogue record for this book is available from the British Library

ISBN: 0 09 182582 2

Designed by Lovelock & Co.

Printed and bound by Sheck Wah Tong Printing Press Ltd

CONTENTS

1 SPRING-CLEAN

You can spend hundreds of hours and thousands of pounds on lotions, potions and treatments to improve the look of your skin, to firm your flesh and to renew your body. But none of these things is likely to bring you the same benefits as simple, natural methods for periodic internal spring-cleaning. Detoxification is just a long word for clearing out your system. A process which stimulates your body's natural ability to get rid of the toxic waste products that build up in your cells, tissues and organs over months and years of living on the Western fare of convenience foods and polluted air. A detox can work miracles after a spate of too much work and too little sleep, after the over-indulgences of Christmas, in spring when all life is renewing itself, before you hit the beach in the summer, or whenever you need a lift.

You might think of spring-cleaning in terms of carting out boxes of junk from the attic. In a way, an internal spring-clean does the same thing. The human body is designed to cleanse itself automatically. The trouble is that the kind of food and drink most people in the West put into their bodies, the tendency we have to lead stressful but sedentary lives, and the increasing number of pollutants to which we are exposed through the air we breathe and the water we drink, have created a situation in which far more toxins are taken into the body, and far more metabolic wastes produced in it, than we can effectively expel. In other words, our bodies are continually having to cope with more poisons than they can eliminate on a normal day-to-day basis. Instead they are stored in the tissues where they lower vitality, encourage the development of degenerative diseases and early ageing and rob the system of nutrients necessary to keep the whole body looking its best.

Garbage Gathering

Dr Dwight McKee, Medical Director of the International Health Institute in America, put it rather bluntly when he said: 'Anybody who has lived the mainstream American lifestyle for ten or more years has seventy trillion garbage cans for cells.' McKee believes, as do a growing number of physicians, that the cells of anyone living in the West are literally chock full of metabolic and environmental wastes gathered over a lifetime. To live at a high level of health and vitality, not to mention being able to make the most of our potential for good looks and prolonged youth, we need to get rid of them.

In order to possess beautiful skin, a firm and healthy body, and a clear mind your system has to be able efficiently and effectively to rid itself of bodily wastes and toxins before they have a chance to do any damage. This principle forms the foundation of the long European tradition of natural medicine. Remove some of the burden of what is creating excess toxicity in your system by laying aside coffee, alcohol, and over-processed foods complete with chemical additives for a time, and you're half-way there. Add to that a very simple and temporary regime designed to trigger rapid detoxification and quite naturally you trigger your body's own mechanisms for clearing out the junk in the attic.

Good Looks from Within

So what do you get out of it? Giving your body the chance to clear out the rubbish it has been carrying around, sometimes for years, will encourage weight loss if there is weight to be shed, will start you on the road to getting rid of cellulite, will improve the look and texture of your skin, minimise lines on your face, improve overall muscle tone, and increase your sense of vitality and well-being. It cleanses the digestive system, restores a good acid/alkaline balance to the body and generally stimulates the proper functioning of organs and tissues. In short, it puts you through the kind of transformation which leaves you sparkling with vitality. Regimes like this keep world-famous health-spas making money hand over foot. Yet you, too, can get that health-spa lift by doing a simple detox in a weekend at home for – believe it or not – the price of a few pounds of apples.

Following such a regime two or three times a year can be enormously helpful in transforming the way you look and feel. The theory is simple. Stop putting into your body those foods which encourage the production of toxic wastes which in turn clog the system. Take two days – a weekend – to relax, spoil yourself, and get your natural elimination processes going by means of an apple fast. Follow that with a few days of taking in lots of delicious living foods to really put you on top form. It's a cheap, effective programme which fits perfectly into a normal working week. Too good to be true? Read on.

2 APPLE MAGIC

A diet always begins tomorrow, and tomorrow it begins the day after that. Because it is hard to find a regime which will fit into your daily routine, it is easy to put it off altogether. This is where the Detox Now programme comes in. It begins with a two-day apple fast, designed to be done over a weekend. It's not even a fast, for you can eat as much as you like – but only apples. For two-days all you have to do is to eat apples, and nothing but apples. Your body will do the rest. The reason why the apple fast is done over a weekend is that the process of elimination can use up a lot of energy so it's a good idea to do it over two-days when you are not working. It is a time to be luxuriously lazy and self-indulgent, and to enjoy the process of getting rid of all those wastes you really don't want hanging around in your system making you look and feel low.

The apple fast was introduced to me thirty years ago by Dr Gordon Latto, a British medical doctor who used nothing but food and breathing techniques and a few herbs to heal even the most complex and chronic conditions. Eating as much as you want – but only apples – in place of your regular meals, and in between too if you like, for two-days cleans your body, helps to clear away food sensitivities, and banishes the ravages of unnatural appetite. A few days on apples once in a while can eliminate retained water, revive flagging energy, make your skin look wonderful and your eyes shine. No pregnant or breast-feeding woman should do an apple fast: neither should anyone with a kidney, liver or heart complaint, for in such cases any sudden change of diet carries with it potential dangers to health. But if you are generally well, a short apple fast is a great way to clear away the cobwebs. Check with your doctor first if you have any doubts.

An Apple a Day

The adage 'an apple a day keeps the doctor away' is not just an old wives' tale. The apple is quite rightly known as the queen of fruits. In its natural whole state it supplies valuable fruit sugar and vitamins in a superb balance to ensure that your body can efficiently digest and use them. The apple is our richest fruit source of vitamin E and also provides a good supply of biotin and folic acid – two B-complex vitamins important in preserving energy, emotional balance and in keeping your digestive system clean and functioning well. It is also a fine source of vitamins A and C which are both natural anti-oxidants – powerful anti-agers – not to mention more than a dozen minerals including sulphur, potassium, iodine, silica, magnesium and calcium, and even essential amino acids in small quantities.

Apples are low in acidity to help balance stored bodily wastes which tend to be acidic. They stimulate the flow of saliva in the mouth and clear away debris from the teeth. Eating a raw fresh apple stimulates circulation in the gums too. Finally, apples are rich in a very special form of soluble fibre called pectin which helps to clear out the dangerous heavy metals such as lead and aluminium that we all pick up from our city air, food and water.

Heavy metals in your body are something you want to get rid of. These elements, the concentration of which has increased dramatically in our air, foods and water since the Industrial Revolution, can seriously interfere with your body's metabolic functioning. Mercury tends to suppress the levels of white blood cells in the immune system. Cadmium displaces the essential element zinc needed for a great many of your body's enzyme systems and renders them inefficient and even inactive. In the West we now have a concentration of lead in our bodies some 500–1000 times that of our pre-industrial ancestors. High levels of this heavy metal age us prematurely, interfere with our mental processes, suppress immunity and contribute to depression. Aluminium, another heavy metal, detrimentally affects the central nervous system. The presence of all these elements in excessive quantities (and their concentrations in the human body appear to be increasing with each passing decade) generally interferes with your body's metabolic processes. The ability of apples to remove heavy metals from your system is one of the best reasons for doing an apple fast, particularly if you live in a city.

Fantastic Fibre

The fibre that apples contain really is remarkable. In addition to cellulose (the most common kind of fibre, which binds water and increases faecal bulk), the apple is also rich in pectin – a very special kind of fibre with quite exceptional detoxification properties. So different in texture and character is pectin from other forms of fibre that it is sometimes surprising to think that they are classified in the same group. Unlike cellulose, pectin does not bind water, it is water soluble. It has no influence on faecal bulking, but it appears to be an excellent substance for lowering cholesterol. It may also help to eliminate bile acids from the intestines, thus short-circuiting the development of colon cancer and gall-stones. It is also useful as a natural chelating (binding) agent which is why it is so good at mopping up unwanted heavy metals such as aluminium from the tissues and eliminating them from the body. This can be very important when it comes to detoxification for weight loss.

Prepare to be Clean

On the day before you have chosen to start your apple fast, go out and buy yourself a big bag of the freshest apples you can find – perhaps three or four different kinds. If you don't like the look of your apples you won't want to eat them, so be picky. Buy a box of apples if you like, your greengrocer might give you a discount.

On this pre-cleanse day it is a good idea to get your system ready. Avoid tea, coffee, alcohol and soft drinks. Steer clear of bread and cooked carbohydrates such as pasta and cereals, and make your last meal of the day a large raw salad made of fresh fruits and vegetables. Don't have anything else to eat after your salad, except perhaps a cup of herb tea before bed. This will give your body a good twelve hours' head-start on the elimination process and it will thank you for it.

The Apple Fast

There's really nothing to it. Over the two-days you have chosen, tuck into your apples. Eat as many as you like at any time of the day or night. You must eat the whole apple, including the peel, the seeds and the core. Chew well, until the last drop of flavour has been extracted from the fruit. The only part you throw away is the woody stem.

Of course, you need to eat your apples raw. You can munch them whole, or grate them and sprinkle a little cinnamon on top. You can even put them in the blender with spring water to make a drink. Eat nothing else during this two-day period, but eat them whenever you are hungry.

Do not drink tea or coffee. You may have herb teas such as

peppermint, lemon balm or camomile with a teaspoon of honey if you wish. Drink lots of spring water, but nothing else.

Be lazy and luxurious. More about this in the next chapter. During these days indulge yourself doing whatever is pleasurable for you. Many people find their sexuality is heightened during these days. If so, enjoy it. Apples are great to munch in bed.

Apple fasting gives you the chance to step back regularly and take a look at your lifestyle, instead of mechanically going on day after day without being aware of where your energy is going. Set aside two days three or four times a year for an apple fast. This will spring-clean your body from the inside out.

Even apple fasting for one day a week is a great boost to vitality and good looks because it helps to detoxify your body of wastes accumulated as a result of drinking or eating too much or consuming the wrong kinds of foods. It can also help to calm the ravages of an over-enthusiastic appetite, which many people suffer as a result of food sensitivities or over-stimulation of the digestive system. Furthermore, it is an excellent discipline: such a practice helps you to break through ingrained habit patterns, which can make you largely unaware of how you are eating.

3 SHEER INDULGENCE

Your two-day apple fast is a not-to-be missed opportunity for some bodily indulgence of the first order. Some of the simplest techniques for supporting your body's elimination processes also happen to feel wonderful and can bring delicious relaxation in their wake. Your body is working hard to get rid of all that stored waste so treat it gently and give it some attention. Your mind will benefit too.

Brush Your Skin

Skin brushing is now frequently recommended by health practitioners and has long been used for health and healing. It is a particularly helpful technique to use during a detox, and can do wonders for your skin if used daily afterwards. Skin brushing acts both superficially, by drawing out wastes from the skin, and deeply by boosting lymphatic drainage (more of this later) and helping to break down congestion in areas where the lymph flow has become sluggish and toxins have collected. It improves the look of the skin, helps to eliminate cellulite, and tones the whole body. It is an extraordinarily gentle yet powerful technique, and it feels wonderful.

Using a natural bristle brush, preferably one with vegetable bristles and a long handle (available from pharmacies, natural beauty shops and health-food stores) go over the surface of your body once with long sweeping motions. Brush across the tops of your shoulders and upper back, then down over your neck and shoulders, down your arms and over your hands – always working in a downward direction and covering the surface of the skin once. Now brush down over your torso and tummy and down your back until you've covered every inch of your upper body. Then, beginning at the feet, brush upwards in the same long, sweeping motions up your legs, front and back, and up over your buttocks. Do this slowly and enjoy feeling the skin of your whole body being gently exfoliated.

Always brush your skin with a dry brush and never brush your face. The amount of pressure you apply should depend on how strong your skin is, your age, and how much stimulation it is used to. Go easy to begin with. Your skin will soon become fitter and then you will be able to work far more vigorously. But you should never go too hard too quickly or it may be counter-productive. Skin brushing encourages better circulation, brings energy to 'deadened' areas of flesh, smoothes and softens the skin, and encourages better lymphatic drainage. You are also sloughing off dead skin cells with the brush, encouraging new cells to come to the surface and making the skin of your whole body glow.

Detox Test

Being your body's largest organ and one of the most important for elimination (almost a third of your body's wastes can be eliminated through the skin), skin that is brushed regularly yields up the most amazing quantity of rubbish. You can check for yourself just how dramatic is the skin's elimination of wastes by performing a practical experiment with the help of a flannel. Every day before your bath or shower, brush your skin all over for three to five minutes. Then take a damp flannel and rub it all over your freshly brushed body. Hang the flannel up and repeat the process with the same flannel the next day. After a few days, the smell of the flannel will be quite revolting thanks to the quantity of waste products that have come directly through the skin's surface. Just think how much better off you are without them.

Balancing Water

After brushing your skin, get into some hydrotherapy – in other words, have a bath. Water is a powerful energy balancer. Water treatments have been used for centuries to help to heal illness and to keep healthy people well. During a two-day detox, water-therapy techniques can help with the elimination process enormously – after all, this is the prefect time for long, relaxing soaks in the bath to soothe your mind and encourage your body to get on with its job.

Epsom-Salts Bath
Epsom-salts baths are an old and potent method of eliminating toxins through the surface of the skin. Epsom salts are magnesium sulphate. Both magnesium and sulphate molecules have an ability to extract excess sodium, phosphorus and nitrogenous toxins from the body. This is why athletes use them to relieve muscular pain. During your apple

fast, having an Epsom-salts bath helps to speed up the detoxification process and minimises any aches, pains or fatigue which sometimes come with eliminating stored toxins rapidly from the body. Epsom salts are also wonderful during periods of prolonged stress and when you are feeling over-tired.

Take two cups of household-grade Epsom salts (available from the chemist), pour them into the bath and fill with blood-temperature water. Immerse yourself for twenty to thirty minutes, topping up with warm water when necessary to maintain a comfortable temperature. Get out of the bath and lie down for fifteen minutes – better still take an Epsom-salts bath just before you go to bed.

The Heat Bath Saunas can be a great help during a detoxification regime as artificially induced perspiration is one of the best means of deep-cleansing the body. However, most of us don't have a sauna at home. You can get a similar effect in terms of the elimination of waste through the skin and deep relaxation by having a carefully regulated hot bath, provided your bath is large enough for you to immerse all of your body except your head in it.

The temperature of the bath is crucial. It needs to be kept at about 40–43°C (105–110°F), i.e., just a few degrees above normal body temperature. Hotter than this can be over-stimulating to the body. You can use a simple thermometer to check the temperature every five minutes and keep topping up with hot water to bring it back when it starts to fall. Lie in the bath for fifteen to twenty minutes with just your head sticking out. Then get out, quickly wrap yourself in a big towel (or a cotton sheet if you prefer) and lie down and relax, covering yourself with a blanket, for another twenty minutes.

Blitzguss A real blitzguss needs to be done by a professional, but you can get many of the same effects in the shower yourself at home, especially if you have a hand-held shower which you can direct onto different parts of your body.

Have a warm shower until your skin is really glowing. Then turn off the hot water and, using only cold, direct it over your face and then down your arms and legs, over your torso and abdomen and down your back. The process should take no more than thirty seconds. Then get out of the shower, pat off the excess water and dress warmly. This is particularly good if done just after skin brushing.

If at any time you feel uncomfortable using any hydrotherapy technique, stop immediately and try again another time. Never force yourself to 'suffer' if any of them cause any tension either in your body or your mind.

Air Bath Water is not the only thing you can bathe in. Of all the nature-cure treatments, the air bath is the simplest. It involves removing all your clothing and allowing fresh air to circulate around your body for a few minutes. It is believed that exposing the body in this way even for only ten minutes can increase metabolism temporarily by as much as fifty per cent, no bad thing when you are trying to eliminate wastes. The easiest way to take a regular air bath is to strip down while you do your morning or evening toilet. Make sure you open a window in the bathroom so that there is fresh air. If you need to turn on a heater in the room do, although cool air on your body for a few minutes can have a positive, stimulating and strengthening effect. This is yet another technique you can use after your two-day apple fast to tone your skin and help to keep that feeling of being fresh and alive that comes after a detox.

4 MOVE UP

We have seen how the skin is a major organ of detoxification and how skin brushing and hydrotherapy can be used to support its work during a two-day apple fast. Now let's take a look at the lungs and the lymphatic system and the help you can give to these main elimination routes during a detox.

Fresh Air

The way you breathe can actually help to clear your system. While the act of breathing is supplying your cells with the oxygen they need, it is also removing carbon dioxide and wastes from your body. In most people, however, this vital process of taking in necessary oxygen and eliminating poisonous wastes is neither as efficient nor as complete as it should be. By far the most common cause of this is simply poor breathing. Most of us use only half our breathing potential and we expel only half the wastes. And, because we don't exhale fully, when we take in new air the old air that is still in the lungs is sucked deeper into them, so the amount of fresh oxygen available to the body is reduced.

The two-day apple fast is a good time to learn about making changes in the way you breathe. Using specific methods of breath control can not only help to detoxify your body but can also increase your energy, calm your emotions, and clear an over-taxed mind. It is a great way to relax.

The Art of the Full Breath

1 When you breathe, breathe with your whole chest and abdomen too. Most of us breathe with only the top part of our body. This kind of restricted breathing stifles emotional expression and is often linked with anxiety, depression and worry. To check for abdominal breathing, lie flat on the floor or on a firm bed and put your hands on your tummy. Does it swell when you breathe in and sink when you breathe out? It should. Lying flat on this firm surface, practise breathing fully and gently until you get the feel of it.

2 Make sure that with each out-breath you let out all the air you have taken in. By exhaling more of the carbon dioxide, you will get rid of more of the cells' waste products and

you will be able to make full use of each new breath of air as it is taken down into your lungs.

3 Be sure to get some exercise – walking, jogging, swimming, trampolining, cycling, dancing or whatever you prefer. Lungs need to be stressed daily in order to function at top peak.

4 Use the following exercise for five minutes twice a day to increase your lung capacity, slim your middle, purify your blood and help you to learn fuller breathing. You can also use it whenever you feel tense or need to clear your head:

Resting your hands on your ribcage at the sides, just above the waist, breathe out completely. Now inhale gently through the nose, letting your abdomen swell as much as it will to a slow count of five. Continue to breathe in through the nose to another count of five, this time letting your ribs expand under your hands and finally your chest too (but don't raise your shoulders in the process). Hold your breath for a count of five, and then let it out through your mouth as you count slowly to ten, noticing how your ribcage shrinks beneath your hands, and pulling in with your abdomen until you have released all the air. Repeat four times.

Lymphomania

None of the body's systems of elimination is less generally recognised or more important than your lymphatic system. Your lymphatic system is not only a major route for the absorption of nutrients and an important carrier of immune cells, it is also your body's metabolic waste-disposal system. So essential are the waste-eliminating functions of the lymphatic system that without them you would die within twenty-four hours. Your lymphatics are a highly organised and elaborate system of ducts and channels which flow all over your body. The opalescent liquid carries wastes and toxic products from these minute channels into larger lymphatic vessels, and on through the lymph nodes which are located in the groin and under the arm and the neck. After being purified by the lymph nodes, the fluid is returned to the blood. In this way the lymphatic system works ceaselessly to clear toxicity.

In many ways the lymph system resembles the blood system. Except in one major respect. Whereas the blood system is powered by the action of the heart, the lymphatic system has no such prime mover. Instead it is almost entirely dependent upon gravity and the natural pressure of muscles when you move your body. These muscle contractions and body movements keep the lymph flowing. For good lymphatic functioning – to keep your body free of the build-up of wastes and toxicity – you need to move your muscles vigorously and often. That is why regular brisk exercise, such as going for long walks, is so important not only to firm your muscles and strengthen your heart and lungs, but also to encourage the steady and effective elimination of wastes from your cells and tissues.

Lymphatic help A particularly pleasant way of helping lymphatic drainage during a two-day apple fast is to lie with your feet higher than your head for a few minutes a couple of times each day. Raise the bottom of your bed 30 cm (a foot) off the floor or lie in a hammock with your feet high. Lying with your feet higher than your head reverses the flow of lymph temporarily, helping to improve lymphatic drainage.

Easy Does It

Nothing produces a holiday high like the right kind of exercise. Exercise is a major detoxifier. It sheds waste and lifts your spirits. And the best kind is the kind you like best. The days of donning pink leg-warmers and busting a gut at the gym because it is supposed to be good for you are over. Exercise is important in the detoxification process as it gets your lungs working and your lymphatic system moving. During your two-day apple fast you need to take some exercise, but only gentle exercise. Long walks are perfect. You do not want to put extra stress on your body by wearing it out with a stiff work-out or long run. If you exercise regularly and are pretty fit then go for a long brisk walk. If exercise is something you would rather not think about, let alone do, indulge yourself in a couple of long, lazy strolls in the park or in the country to get your lungs and lymph working efficiently.

Rebound Madness

Rebounding (bouncing up and down on a mini-trampoline) is tremendous, childish fun. This is probably reason enough to do it, but it is also a brilliant aid to detoxification. The unique up-and-down movement of your body on a mini-trampoline subjects it to changes in gravitational force. For a split second at the top of the bounce, gravity or G-force is non-existent. But at the bottom of each bounce, as you come down upon the elastic platform, the pull of gravity on your cells, muscles and tissues is suddenly increased by two or even three times the usual G-force on the earth. On the way up, gravity closes up the millions of one-way valves which control the flow of lymph. Then when you come down again onto the trampoline, the internal pressure changes quickly and dramatically, causing the valves to open and bringing about a surge of lymph so you set up an internal massaging motion which shunts lymph along.

Rebounding is the perfect solution for anyone who wants to exercise at home, no matter what their fitness level. It's particularly good for anyone who is embarrassed by the idea of going out in running gear or going to the gym. Unlike many in-the-home exercise options, rebounding has a particularly high continued-use success rate, probably because it is so much fun. It gets your mind and body working and seems to raise spirits like nothing else I have ever come across. I often use it for ten minutes or so when I'm feeling fatigued or stressed.

Begin bouncing gently so that your heels barely leave the ground. If you feel unsteady, use the back of a chair to support yourself with one arm as you bounce. You might like to bounce to music or even while watching television. As an alternative to bouncing with both feet together, try jogging from one foot to the other. Begin doing ten minutes a day and work up to thirty minutes or so as your strength increases.

Walk it Out

Regular aerobic exercise (where your heart is beating firmly and you breathe deeply over a period of thirty–forty-five minutes) is essential to long-term health. It increases your body's ability to process oxygen, and a high consumption of oxygen keeps your energy high and keeps you looking and feeling good. Moreover, exercise can be as good for your mind as it can for your body. And, just in case you think you have to become a marathon runner, you may be surprised to find our how simple real fitness can be.

Brisk daily walks can not only be a lot of fun, they can help to keep your body clean from the inside out. Start slowly if you are not used to exercise and then gradually – over several weeks if necessary – work up your pace to six kilometres (four miles) an hour. This means you will be walking a mile in about fifteen minutes. Once you can do that easily you will be able to walk, say, five kilometres (three miles) a day in forty-five minutes and you'll be getting a very pleasant but effective workout which will bring you lots of energy and make you feel great.

Of course, there are other alternatives as well – you could swim or jog or skip or row. (Before undertaking any sort of exercise, it is advisable to see your doctor for a health check.) Each of these requires special equipment and special places and times, whereas walking can be done almost anywhere by anyone without any special training and without spending extra money.

5 CLEANSING HELP

Very occasionally when someone goes on an active programme of detoxification, such as an apple fast for a few days, they may experience a severe headache, feel moody, or have an upset stomach, a film on their tongue or teeth, even loose bowels. These are signs that your body is throwing off wastes at such a pace that you are experiencing what is known in natural medicine as a cleansing crisis.

In reality it happens to very few people. If you are one of them, remember that it is actually a good sign. Your body is taking the opportunity you have afforded it through what you are eating (and what you are not eating) of throwing off a lot of debris. Take the time to relax, lie down in a darkened room if possible, and be kind to yourself. Have a cup of peppermint tea, which is very soothing when you have a headache. If you can't sleep, try a cup of camomile tea, or eat a banana which is rich in the amino acid tryptophan, a superb natural sedative. It will pass quickly, leaving you better than ever.

Caffeine Trouble

The people most likely to get a headache as part of a cleansing crisis are those who habitually drink several cups of coffee or tea a day. This reaction is triggered by your tissues dumping a lot of stored caffeine into your bloodstream all at once in order to eliminate it from your body. But when it passes you should have the most wonderful feeling of freshness and lightness. This sense of lightness is a common one for people who for the first time begin to clear their system of stored wastes. It more than makes up for the headache or upset stomach which can herald its coming.

Clever Compress

Something I learnt many years ago from a doctor who uses natural methods for healing, is that in a cleansing crisis you can help your body by putting a simple cool compress around your middle and leaving it there while you lie down for half an hour. This can also be done when you go to bed in the evening if you prefer. A cool compress stimulates the flow of blood to the area of the liver – another prime mover when it comes to detoxification – so speeding up the release of wastes from the body and easing any unpleasant symptoms that come with them. Using a compress is also enormously relaxing.

Tear a piece of cotton fabric (an old sheet is ideal) into a rectangular piece about 38 cm (15 in) wide and long enough to fit comfortably around the middle of your body (between your armpits and hips). Wet this compress in cold water and wring it out completely so it is only damp. Now, using a dry towel (or a piece of wool or thick natural fabric) which is also big enough to go around your middle and to overlap so that you can pin it comfortably with a few safety-pins, spread the compress out on the outstretched towel. Place your naked midriff on this strip and wrap first the compress around you and then the towel, pinning it securely. Pull your clothes or nightclothes down over the lot and pop into a warm bed for at least half an hour. Such a compress can help you not only to get through a cleansing crisis, but also if you ever find it difficult to sleep because of worry or stress.

Kidney Power

If you find yourself experiencing some uncomfortable symptoms during your apple fast, increase the quantity of spring water you are drinking. When the body's water level gets too low, the kidneys don't work efficiently and the liver has to take on too much of the cleansing work on its own. If you tend to retain water this is often because you don't drink enough so your body tries its best to hold on to the water there is in order to dilute any toxicity in your tissues.

Believe it or not you breathe out about two big glasses-worth of water a day. The kidneys and intestines eliminate roughly another six glasses and two are released through the skin. So keep drinking – during a detox and afterwards. We all tend to need more water than we drink for optimum health. It's a good idea to keep a bottle or two of mineral water on your desk or somewhere where you will see it often to remind you to take in enough water each day.

Here is a simple formula for working out the ideal quantity of water to drink each day for maximum energy and good looks. Divide your current weight in kilos by 8.

(e.g., 58 kilos divided by 8 = 7.25). Round the figure up (to 8) and that is the number of glasses of water you need each day.

This is just a base calculation, of course. Drinking enough water is one of the most important things you can do to keep your body eliminating wastes efficiently. Remember that you will probably need to take in more water than your base calculation when you are exercising or if the weather is hot.

Psychic Detox

Some people can get a temporary feeling of let-down on a detox. This is usually because the heart, having been stimulated by caffeine and other irritants, begins to beat more slowly and the false exhilaration you used to get from stimulants temporarily turns into a feeling of being down. It doesn't last long, and in most people it doesn't happen at all.

Sometimes, all sorts of psychic junk suddenly gets released along with the physical toxins you have been carrying around. Feelings of anxiety, worry or guilt may surface for no apparent reason. Fear not; they will most likely just be flushed away with all the other junk your body is getting rid of. In the meantime, try putting a few drops of lavender or vanilla essential oil in an oil burner or in your bath and breathe in the fragrance.

One of the nice things about this sort of detox is that you often find that you think much more clearly after it. Stress does many unpleasant things to the body, one of which is that it can make your whole system acidic. An apple fast alkalinises your system, bringing it back into balance and throwing off the by-products of stress in the process. When you are mentally stressed your body becomes physically stressed through having to deal with all this toxic waste. Removing these toxic wastes can often improve your ability to deal with more stress. You begin to see things in a much more positive light and can put what once seemed difficult problems into their proper perspective.

Relax and Revive

During a detox it is important to make sure you get enough rest. Think how good you feel after a holiday. It's usually the one time when you actually allow yourself to rest – something you don't do enough of during the rest of the year. Rest is essential because it is while you are at rest that your tissues restore themselves. During a detox your body is working pretty hard in eliminating all the rubbish you have allowed to be released into your system, so relax and don't feel guilty about it. Watch your favourite videos, read that book you've been promising yourself you'll find time for, listen to all your old records, or just do nothing. This is a precious time, a time to devote to yourself and your body's needs. Don't waste it.

During the day, whenever you can, lie down even for ten minutes and just let go. Or practise a simple relaxation/mediation exercise like this one:

Close your eyes and watch your breath coming in and out of your body. With each out breath count silently. So it goes like this: 'In breath …out breath …one …in breath …out breath …two …' and so on up to ten. If you lose track or find that your mind is distracted it doesn't matter at all. Just go back to 'one' and start again.

Carry this out for ten to fifteen minutes whenever you can find a few spare minutes to yourself. It helps to rebalance your body's nervous system and can be useful if you have to deal with any negative emotions that surface during your detox.

6 BREAK-FAST

The way that you choose to eat after an apple fast is vitally important. If you break your fast the wrong way, all the benefits of eating only apples for two-days will be lost. Having got rid of the junk, you don't want to put any more in.

The first two or three days after your apple fast you should eat only raw food – particularly fruit. Don't eat too much, chew your food well and eat slowly. This is good advice for anyone at any time. Putting too much of even the very best food into your system will lower your energy, because so much of your energy goes into digesting and assimilating excess food and eliminating the wastes which are by-products of metabolising it. Don't eat when you are not hungry and stop as soon as you feel full.

Remarkably Raw

Raw foods have a remarkable ability to rebalance and restore the entire body. At the same time a high-raw diet provides a full complement of essential vitamins, minerals and amino acids in an easily assimilable form. This means that, unlike a crash diet which depletes your body of the nutrients it needs and leaves you tired and irritable, an apple fast followed by a few days on raw fruits and vegetables will give you lots of energy. For the first three days you will do best to eat something like this:

Breakfast Live Muesli or Energy Shake (see pages 48–51).

Mid-Morning A glass of fresh vegetable or fruit juice, or herb tea with a little honey to sweeten if you wish. Avoid coffee, tea, alcohol and soft drinks.

Lunch For an appetiser have slices of fresh fruit such as apple, mango or melon. Follow with a large raw salad (see page 51).

Dinner Begin with a freshly-squeezed raw vegetable juice cocktail, or half a grapefruit. For a main course have another big raw salad with fresh fruit for desert.

On the fourth day you can begin to add a little more cooked food, such as homemade lentil soup with a slice of wholemeal bread and a salad for lunch, or a piece of fresh fish or chicken with a salad for dinner. Each of us is different so it's important to listen to your body's needs. Be sure to eat enough at each meal, but don't stuff yourself. If you get hungry between meals have a piece of fresh fruit or some sunflower seeds. This is not a starvation diet. There is no need to cheat.

After your detox and a few days on raw foods you will probably want to keep that wonderful feeling of clean and fresh vitality. To do this you need to cut out the rubbish that you have been taking in such as convenience foods and highly-processed foods, including breakfast cereals, bread made from refined flour, white pasta, white sugar and all the 'goodies' made from it. Choose organic tea or coffee to avoid taking in any more chemicals and pesticides than absolutely necessary. Drink no more than a cup or two a day. Don't drink too much alcohol – have only a glass (or occasionally two at the most) of good wine with a meal once a day. And remember to drink plenty of spring water.

Take in foods which support the proper functioning of your body's natural elimination processes, and remember not to overload your system in the morning when your liver is working hard. Try to eat half of your foods raw. Eat lots of natural foods, such as fresh fruits and vegetables, pulses and nuts, and smaller quantities of steamed or wok-fried fish, game and poultry. If this sounds boring, think again. At the end of the chapter you will find a few ideas and recipes to set you on the way to eating delicious and wholesome foods that will help you to avoid putting back into your system all that junk you have just got rid of. Lots of fresh, wholesome fruits and vegetables, prepared simply so you keep all of their wonderful tastes and textures are delicious. Go and see what your greengrocer has on offer and let your imagination run riot.

Sprout Magic

Ensure your meals are crammed with goodness by sprouting your own seeds (sometimes called bean sprouts). Seeds and grains are latent powerhouses of nutritional goodness and life energy. Add water to germinate them, let them grow for a few days in your kitchen and you will harvest delicious, inexpensive fresh foods of quite phenomenal health-enhancing value. The vitamin content of seeds increases dramatically when they germinate. Some sprouted seeds and grains are believed to have anti-cancer properties which is why they form an important part of the natural methods of treating the disease. Another attractive thing about sprouts is their price. The basic seeds and grains are cheap and readily available in supermarkets and health-food stores – chickpeas, brown lentils, mung beans, wheat grains and so forth. And since you sprout them yourself with nothing but clean water, they become an easily accessible source of organically-grown fresh vegetables, even for city dwellers. Make them the base for salads, add them at the last minute to homemade soups, even carry them around with you in a bag and eat them instead of chocolate bars and biscuits. They are sweet and delicious and won't leave you with an energy slump. Information on how to sprout your own seeds and grains is given at the end of this chapter.

Dessert Desert? No Way

Many people think that eating healthily means giving up all the things they like, such as sweet things and desserts. This is not true; just take a look at some of the recipes that follow. Most people make the mistake of thinking that sugar gives them energy. True, sugar is high in calories, but these are largely empty. The energy jolt you feel after eating a bar of chocolate comes from the sugar flooding your bloodstream, which triggers the release of insulin. It is the job of insulin to keep things in balance, so it encourages the sugar not to be burned as energy, but rather to be stored as fat, thus reducing the level of your blood sugar. So, quick as a flash, your energy vanishes.

Unfortunately, frequent sugar-eaters' bodies tend to over-react and lower the blood sugar too much. This is why the familiar (and very short-lived) lift in mood and energy which comes from eating something sugary is soon followed by a depressive slump which can send you reaching for more sugar in a vicious cycle of fatigue and the effort to combat it. To avoid this high-low reaction and up-and-down cycle, steer clear of all refined carbohydrates – from sugar to white flour – and anything made from them. Instead, choose complex carbohydrates, such as fruit, vegetables and wholemeal breads and cereals which release just the right kind of energy into your bloodstream slowly, bringing you sustained energy and enormous staying power.

Eating sugar also robs your body of chromium, an important mineral which helps to protect against chronic low blood sugar and fatigue. Studies show that chromium deficiencies are common in Britain and the United States, in part because we eat so much refined sugar and in part as a result of agricultural practices which have depleted our soils of the mineral. Eat raw fruits and vegetables that have been grown organically and you will be replacing all sorts of minerals lost through a diet of convenience foods.

Potassium Power

Potassium is another important mineral for keeping your body's elimination processes working properly on a daily basis. One of its jobs is to look after the activity of your nerves and muscles, and when too little of it is available you can become lethargic, weary and weak. It plays an important part in ensuring that your cells receive the oxygen and nutrients they need and that their wastes are properly eliminated. Potassium is easily lost from your body. This means you need a fresh supply through your foods every day. Two factors contribute to potassium deficiency. First, potassium and sodium are antagonists which should balance each other in your body. Thanks to all the salt added to convenience foods and used at the table to season foods, many people eat a high-sodium diet. Then sodium gets the upper hand, potassium levels drop and you can end up chronically fatigued. Low potassium levels also result from our Western tendency to eat too few fresh fruits and vegetables, which are high in potassium.

The best way to take in potassium is to take in lots of fresh fruits and vegetables, their juices and homemade vegetable soups. Also, stop seasoning your food with salt. There is plenty of natural sodium in wholesome foods without adding more. Three weeks of eating like this can dramatically heighten your energy levels and increase your over-all feeling of health.

Go For It

The following are some ideas of how to put together delicious meals that will keep your body working well and your energy levels high. Try them out, then make up your own. There's a whole world of possibilities out there.

Bountiful Breakfasts A traditional cooked breakfast

of fried eggs, bacon, toast with butter and jam and tea or coffee is definitely bad news. In the first place, greasy food puts a great strain on your liver, which is working hardest to detoxify your body between midnight and midday, and its high fat content will leave you tired and mentally dull. Far better to choose an energising breakfast such as Live Muesli, or an Energy Shake, or just fresh fruit.

Live Muesli

This recipe is similar to the original muesli developed by the famous Swiss physician, Max Bircher-Benner. Unlike packaged muesli, which usually contains too much sugar and is rather heavy and hard to digest, the bulk of this muesli is made up of fresh fruit. It will leave you feeling light and lively.

1–2 heaped tablespoons of oat, rye or wheat flakes
a handful of raisins or sultanas
1 apple or firm pear, grated or diced
1 teaspoon of fresh orange or lemon juice
1 small banana, finely chopped
2 tablespoons of yoghurt (optional)
1 teaspoon of honey or unsulphured blackstrap molasses or

concentrated fruit juice (optional)
1 tablespoon of chopped nuts or sunflower seeds
½ teaspoon of powdered cinnamon or ginger

Soak the grain flakes overnight in a little water or fruit juice to help to break the starch down, along with the raisins or sultanas. In the morning, combine the soaked grain flakes and raisins with the apple or pear and banana, add the orange or lemon juice to prevent the fruit from browning and to aid digestion. Top with the yoghurt, then drizzle with honey, molasses or concentrated fruit juice if you like. Sprinkle with chopped nuts or sunflower seeds and spices.

You can prepare countless variations of Live Muesli by using different types of fresh fruit, such as strawberries, peaches, pitted cherries or pineapple, depending on what's in season. When your choice of fresh fruit is limited, use soaked dried fruit such as apricots, dates, more sultanas, figs or pears.

Energy Shake
This recipe is delightful and quick – ideal if you have little time to spare in the mornings.

225 ml (8 fl oz/1 cup) plain yoghurt
a handful of strawberries or raspberries
1 teaspoon of honey or unsulphured blackstrap molasses
1 tablespoon of coconut (optional)
a squeeze of lemon juice

Combine all the ingredients thoroughly in a blender or food processor and drink. Depending on the type of yoghurt used, you may need to thin the shake with a little fruit juice. As with Live Muesli you can vary the Energy Shake by using different kinds of fruit, such as bananas, mango or fresh pineapple.

Sexy Salads

Most people think of a salad as a rather limp affair involving a few bits of lettuce and some cucumber. What I mean by a salad is a taste sensation of fresh, raw vegetables presented beautifully and dressed to kill. The permutations are endless. Go for the freshest vegetables in season and let your creative (and digestive) juices run riot. Here's one of my recipes to get you started:

Line a large dish with lettuce or spinach leaves. Then chop or grate a selection of fresh vegetables and fruit, such as cabbage (red or white), carrots, radishes, tomatoes, courgettes, cauliflower, broccoli, green peppers, apples, beetroot, cucumber, oranges or grapes. Add a handful of sprouted seeds or beans such as alfalfa, mung, chickpeas or lentils. Dress with a little extra-virgin olive oil, a squeeze of fresh orange or lemon juice, a little curry powder, ginger or a dash or Worcester Sauce, and a little Swiss Vegetable Bouillon Powder to taste. Top the lot with a handful of sunflower seeds or chopped nuts.

To your basic salad you can add a side-dish of grated boiled egg, a little chicken or fish, or some brown rice or a baked potato. Make plenty and you won't go hungry.

Sweet Treats

Raspberry Fruit Freeze Pie
This is a great basic pie base that you can fill with any fruits and berries that are in season. Here is my favourite:

Pie Base:
1 cup of pitted dried dates
½ cup of almonds

¼ cup of oat flakes
1 teaspoon of honey
a little water

Grind the dates and almonds as finely as possible in a food processor. Add the oats, honey and a little water and blend again. You need to add the water slowly to get the right consistency. You want the mixture to bind but not be sticky, so that it rolls into a ball in the food processor. Flatten the mixture into a pie dish with your fingers or the back of a wooden spoon. As a variation you can add a tablespoon or two of coconut.

Pie Filling:
2 bananas
2 cups of raspberries
sherry
honey to sweeten

Peel the bananas and chop them into pieces about 2½ cm (1 in) thick. Freeze in a polythene bag with the raspberries until firm. Remove from the freezer and blend the fruits together with a dash of sherry and a little honey to sweeten if you like. Pour into the pie crust and serve immediately, garnished with a few banana slices or raspberries.

Carob and Apple Cake

 1 cup of sunflower seeds (or a 2:1 mixture of sunflower
   and sesame seeds)
 1 cup of carob powder
 ½ cup of dried coconut
 ½ cup of dried pitted dates
 3 apples
 ½ teaspoon of vanilla essence
 1 teaspoon of allspice
 apple slices or strawberries to garnish

Grind the seeds very finely. Add the carob powder, coconut and dates. Quarter and core the apples, then blend them in the food processor with the dry ingredients. Add the vanilla essence and allspice. Spoon the mixture into a flat dish and leave to chill for a couple of hours in the fridge. Decorate with apple and/or strawberry slices before serving.

Carob Fudge

Once chilled, these wonderful fudge balls have the texture of ordinary fudge, and their carob flavour makes them ideal chocolate substitutes.

1 cup of sesame seeds
½ cup of dried coconut
½ cup of carob powder
1 teaspoon of honey
½ teaspoon of vanilla essence

Grind the seeds very finely in the food processor. Add the other ingredients and process again. Form the mixture into little balls and chill.

DIY Sprouting When you discover how economical and easy it is to grow sprouts, you will want to have some on the go all the time. Once germinated you can keep sprouts in polythene bags in the fridge for up to a week – just long enough to get a new batch ready for eating. Most people grow sprouts in glass jars covered with nylon mesh held in place with an elastic band around the neck, but I have discovered an even simpler method which allows you to grow many more and avoids the jar method problem of seeds rotting due to insufficient drainage.

You will need the following:
seeds (e.g., mung beans)
seed trays with drainage holes, available from gardening shops and nurseries
a jar or bowl to soak seeds in overnight
a plant atomiser, from gardening or hardware shops
a sieve
nylon mesh, available from gardening shops

1 Place two handfuls of seeds or beans in the bottom of a jar or bowl and cover with plenty of water. Leave to soak overnight.
2 Pour the seeds into a sieve and rinse well with water. Remove any dead or broken seeds or pieces of debris.
3 Line a seedling tray with nylon mesh (this helps the seeds

to drain better) and pour in the soaked seeds.
4 Place in a warm, dark spot for fast growth.
5 Spray the seeds twice a day with fresh water in an atomiser and stir them gently with your hand in order to aerate them.
6 After about three days, place the seeds in sunlight for several hours to develop the chlorophyll (green) in them.
7 Rinse in a sieve, drain well and put in a polythene bag. Refrigerate and use in salads, wok-fries, etc.

There are many different seeds you can sprout – each with its own particular flavour and texture. Use the following chart as a guide.

SPROUTING

Seeds	Soak time	To Yield 1 litre	Ready to eat in
Alfalfa	6–8 hours	3–4 tbsp	5–6 days
Fenugreek	6–8 hours	1½ cups	3–4 days
Adzuki beans	10–15 hours	1½ cups	3–5 days
Chickpeas	10–15 hours	2 cups	3–4 days
Lentils	10–15 hours	1 cup	3–5 days
Mung beans	15 hours	1 cup	3–5 days
Sunflower seeds	10–15 hours	4 cups	1–2 days
Wheat	12–15 hours	2 cups	2–3 days

Length of shoot	Growing tips and notes
3.5 cm/1½ in	Rich in organic vitamins and minerals
1 cm/½ in	Have quite a strong 'curry' taste. Good for ridding the body of toxins
2.5–3.5 cm/1–1½ in	Have a nutty flavour. Especially good for the kidneys
2.5 cm/1 in	May need to soak for 18 hrs to swell to their full size. Replace the water during this time
0.5-2.5cm/½–1 in	Try all different kinds of lentils. They are good eaten young or up to 6 days old
1–5 cm/½–2½ in	Keep in the dark for a sweet sprout
Same length as seed	Sprout for just a day. Bruise easily so handle carefully
Same length as grain	An excellent source of the B vitamins. The soak water can be drunk straight or added to soups and vegetable juices

RESOURCES

More from Leslie Kenton

Leslie lectures and teaches workshops throughout the world on health, authentic power, energy, creativity, shamanism, and spirituality. Two companies organise workshops for her in Britain: Bright Ideas provides workshops on health, energy and personal empowerment and books Leslie for lectures and individually-tailored seminars when these are requested. (For further ideas contact Bright Ideas: Telephone (in the UK) 08700 783783, or e-mail **LK@bright-idea.co.uk**) The Sacred Trust organises Leslie's residential and non-residential workshops on freedom, spirituality, creativity and shamanism. For further information contact The Sacred Trust, PO Box 603, Bath BA1 2ZU: Telephone 01225 852615, Fax 01225 858961.

Leslie's audio tapes including *10 Steps to a New You*, as well as her videos including *10 Day Clean Up Plan*, *Ageless Ageing*, *Lean Revolution*, *10 Day De-Stress Plan*, and *Cellulite Revolution*, can be ordered from QED Recording Services Ltd, Lancaster Road, New Barnet, Hertfordshire, EN4 8AS. Telephone 0181 441 7722, Fax 0181 441 0777, e-mail **lesliekenton@qed-productions.com**

If you want to know about Leslie's personal appearances, forthcoming books, videos, workshops and projects please visit her website for the latest information: **http://www.qed-productions/lesliekenton.htm**

You can also write to her care of QED at the above address enclosing a stamped, self-addressed A4 sized envelope.

Suppliers:

The Soil Association
The Organic Food & Farming Centre, 86 Coulson Street, Bristol BS1 5BB
Write to them for their regularly updated National Directory of Farm Shops and Box Schemes.

Organics Direct
1-7 Willow Street, London EC2A 4BH
Telephone 0171 729 2828. Or visit their website on
http://www.organicsdirect.com. You can also order online.

Organics Direct offers a nationwide home delivery service of fresh vegetables and fruits, delicious breads, juices, sprouts, fresh soups, ready-made meals, snacks and baby foods. They even sell organic wines – all shipped to you within 24 hours.

Essential Oils: Top-quality aromatherapy products are available from *Sandra Day*, Ashley House, 185A Drake Street, Rochdale, Lancashire 0L11 1E7: Telephone 01706 750302, Fax 01706 750 304. Tisserand do an essential-oil diffuser that plugs in and fans the oils into the air. Contact *Tisserand Aromatherapy*, Newtown Road, Hove, Sussex BN3 7BA: Telephone 01273 325 666.

Index